GUIDE TO
AUSTRALIA

MICHAEL MARCH

Highlights for Children

CONTENTS

On the cover: The Opera House in Sydney, with its roof built to look like boat sails caught in the wind above the harbor

Published by Highlights for Children

© 1995 Highlights for Children, Inc.
P. O. Box 18201
Columbus, Ohio 43218-0201

10 9 8 7 6 5 4

ISBN 0-87534-914-5

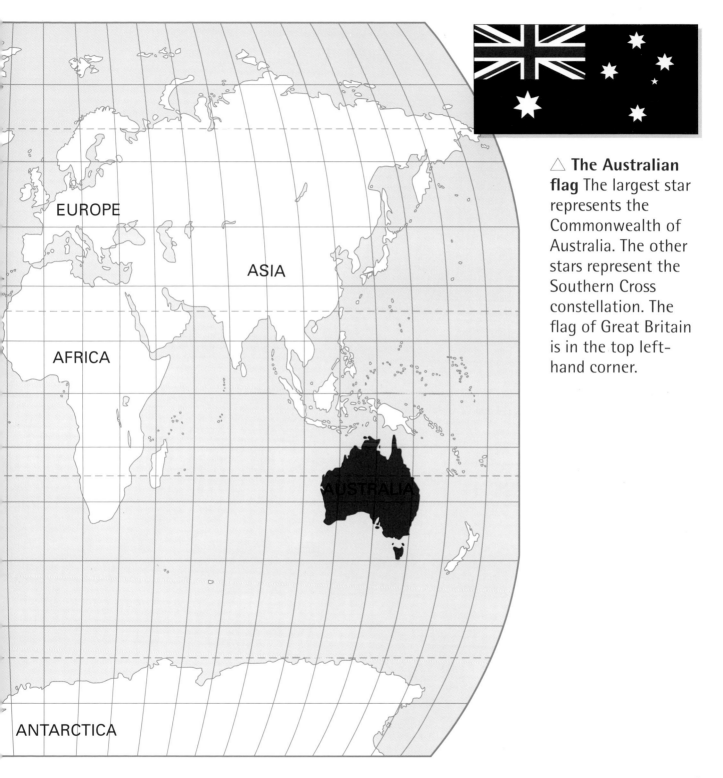

EUROPE

ASIA

AFRICA

AUSTRALIA

ANTARCTICA

△ **The Australian flag** The largest star represents the Commonwealth of Australia. The other stars represent the Southern Cross constellation. The flag of Great Britain is in the top left-hand corner.

AUSTRALIA AT A GLANCE

Area 2,966,200 square miles
(7,682,300 square kilometers)
Population 17,800,000
Capital Canberra, population
310,000
Other big cities Sydney
(3,719,000), Melbourne
(3,187,000)
Highest mountain Mt. Kosciusko
7,316 feet (2,230 meters)
Longest river Murray 1,609 miles
(2,590 kilometers)
Largest lake Lake Eyre 3,700
square miles (9,600 square
kilometers)
Official language English

▽ **Australian postage stamps** Some celebrate historical events, others feature sports, Australia's wildlife, and the International Year of the Family.

◁ **Australian money** has cents and dollars. These bills feature famous Australians, such as poet Dame Mary Gilmore and humanitarian "Flynn of the Inland."

120°E 125°E 130°E 135°E 140°E 145°E 150°E 155°E

N E S I A

O C E A N

New Guinea

N
W E
S

10°S

•Darwin

Gulf of
Carpentaria

Coral Sea

15°S

Great
Sandy Desert

NORTHERN

TERRITORY

•Cairns

Great Barrier Reef

Great Dividing Range

20°S

Gibson Desert

QUEENSLAND

Tropic of Capricorn

WESTERN

Alice
Springs•

25°S

AUSTRALIA

▲ Uluru

Great Victoria Desert

Lake
Eyre

SOUTH

AUSTRALIA

•Brisbane

NEW

Darling

30°S

•Perth

Great

Australian Bight

SOUTH

WALES

Murray

Murrumbidgee

•Sydney

Adelaide•

Canberra★✈

VICTORIA

▲ Mt. Kosciusko

35°S

Melbourne•

Tasman

TASMANIA

Sea

40°S

•Hobart

AUSTRALIA

| | Farmland & Forest |
| | Desert |

★ Capital
● Major Cities
▲ Mountain Peaks
— State Boundaries

0 100 200 300 Miles
0 200 400 Kilometers

© Oxford Cartographers

5

"DOWN UNDER"

Australia is an island-continent that lies between the Pacific and Indian Oceans. Much of the land is grassland and stony desert. The country is very dry and very flat. A chain of low mountains, called the Great Dividing Range, stretches down the east coast.

Australians sometimes call their homeland "down under" because it is south of the Equator. "Down under," the seasons occur at opposite times of the year to those north of the Equator. People sunbathe on the beach, or go surfing, on Christmas Day. They go snow skiing in the middle of July. In the tropical north, nearly all the rain falls early in the year, during the "wet season." Powerful storms called cyclones can strike without warning. Flooding and droughts are common throughout the year.

Australia is a large country in area, but only about 18 million people live here. Most of them live in the south or along the southeast coasts. Australia's first people, the Aborigines, have been here more than 40,000 years. The Aboriginal population is now very small. Some Australians are descendants of convicts who were sent here from Great Britain 200 years ago. Later, Americans, Chinese, and others came to pan for gold. Many of them stayed. Since then, people from all parts of the world have settled here.

Australia is a land of great natural beauty. You can explore coral reefs, rain forests, and vast deserts. You can visit sheep stations (large farms) that cover thousands of acres. In the wild countryside, called the bush, you will see grazing kangaroos and other fascinating animals. You can travel around Australia by bus and train, and airplanes fly between cities and towns. But to explore the outback — the great interior wilderness — you can use a four-wheel-drive vehicle or fly in a small airplane.

▽ **Aborigine children** There are about 170,000 Aborigines in Australia. Some still hunt in the outback, as their ancestors used to do. But most live in towns and cities.

▽ **North Stradbroke Island, near Brisbane** People come here for the surfing and sandy beaches. Dolphins and porpoises swim in these waters.

◁ **A fruit farm in Queensland** Fruits, such as mangoes, pineapples, and papayas, are grown here. Houses are built on blocks to allow the cool air to flow beneath them.

THE FIRST CITY

Sydney is Australia's largest and oldest city. It was started by settlers who arrived on the southeast coast of Australia in 1788. Many of these men and women were convicts from Britain. They were sent to Australia to serve their sentences because the jails in Britain were full. Some years earlier, Captain Cook of the British navy had explored Botany Bay, near where Sydney Airport is today. But the convict ships finally dropped anchor a little farther north of Botany Bay, in what is now called Sydney Harbor. The fleet commander, Captain Arthur Phillip, described it as "one of the finest natural harbors in the world."

▽ **Vineyards in Hunter Valley, north of Sydney** Grapes for fine wines are grown here. Coal is also mined in the valley.

△ **Café at Bondi Beach** Bondi is Sydney's most popular beach. It is famous for its surfing. Surfers and swimmers are kept apart for safety, and nets stop sharks from coming too close.

◁ **Sydney Tower** From the observation gallery at the top, you can see as far as the Blue Mountains to the west. There is also a revolving restaurant 1,000 feet (305 meters) above the ground.

A trip around Sydney Harbor is a must. Skyscrapers rise above the busy port. Here, container ships are loaded and unloaded. Ocean liners, passenger ferries, and sailing boats come and go. Sailing west, you pass under the great steel arch of Sydney Harbor Bridge. The bridge spans 1,653 feet (503 meters) and connects the northern and southern parts of the city. Just below the bridge, on the southern side, is the city's old quarter. This is where the early settlers lived. Opposite, Sydney Opera House juts out into the harbor. The opera house is shaped like the billowing sails of a huge yacht.

In town, you can buy moleskins, thick cotton pants like those worn by the farmers in the outback. You can also find other souvenirs of Australia such as kangaroo-hide belts or Aboriginal tree-bark paintings. Restaurants offer a wide choice, including crawfish, hamburgers, Turkish kebabs, and Japanese sushi. Outside the city, you can visit the beautiful Blue Mountains. The rough terrain is covered with eucalyptus trees, and waterfalls tumble down steep cliffs.

CAPITAL CITY

The flight from Sydney to Canberra takes only half an hour. Although Canberra is much smaller than Sydney, it is Australia's capital. Since 1927, the government, or parliament, has met here. Canberra is a modern city of broad, tree-lined avenues and big public parks and gardens. At its center is Lake Burley Griffin. This is a man-made lake, named for the American who designed the city. The old parliament building stands at the foot of a hill on the south side of the lake. The new parliament building overlooks the city from the top of the same hill.

△ **An Australian sheep station** The sheep are the hardy merino breed, which produce the world's finest wool.

From Canberra, the road south crosses a plain where huge flocks of sheep graze the yellow-brown grass. Sheep were brought to Australia by the early settlers. Today, there are more sheep in Australia than there are people. Farther on is the old town of Cooma, known as the gateway to the Snowy Mountains, or Australian Alps. Twenty-seven national flags fly in Cooma. They represent the nationalities of the people who helped build the Snowy Mountains Hydroelectric System. Tunnels were dug under the mountains and dams built on the Snowy and Murrumbidgee Rivers. The water behind the dams drives turbines to make electricity.

In midwinter, you can go skiing in the Snowy Mountains. In summer, the mountains are covered in flowers. You can hike or go horseback riding here, and you can fish in the streams. A chairlift takes you close to the top of Mount Kosciusko, Australia's highest mountain. Much farther north, on the New England Plateau, you can see a burning mountain. Smoke rises from coal that was lit deep underground, perhaps by lightning, a thousand years ago.

◁ **The Australian flag flying over the new Parliament House, Canberra** The building was opened in 1988. It is designed as part of Capital Hill, and the roof is covered with grass.

▷**Perisher Valley Ski Resort, in the Snowy Mountains** Between July and September, the only time it snows here, skiers flock to this resort.

THE SUNSHINE STATE

Like Sydney, Brisbane began as a convict settlement. Today, it is the capital of the state of Queensland, and more than a million people live here. On the oldest street, you will find a modern shopping center, with glass elevators and an indoor roller coaster. At ground level there are street musicians and acrobats. Brisbane's oldest building is known as the Observatory. It was once a mill. Long ago convicts worked here from morning until night grinding corn.

▽ **Mining at Mount Isa** Tall smokestacks, giant slag heaps, and thousands of mining trucks are spread over a huge area.

◁ **Kangaroos and wallabies at Currumbin Sanctuary, near the Gold Coast** Koalas, emus, and other Australian animals live here in the natural bush and lakes.

Southeast of Brisbane are the scenic long beaches of the Gold Coast. Surfing and sunbathing are popular here. The sun shines 300 days a year in this part of Queensland. But farther inland the climate is very different. You can walk through rain forest so thick that few of the sun's rays ever reach the forest floor. Sometimes you hear wallabies in the undergrowth. At dusk, you might see a duck-billed platypus feeding in a creek.

As you travel west the land becomes drier. But the soil is rich in minerals. The little town of Roma, in the scrubland of Queensland's Central Highlands, has its own oil and gas fields. In Anakie Fields, to the north, you can try searching for sapphires. Sometimes, when the dusty soil is flooded by rain, precious stones can be seen sparkling in the mud.

Mount Isa is a distant town in the outback. There are huge copper, lead, and silver mines here. You can borrow a miner's hat and overalls and explore some of the many miles of underground tunnels.

◁ **Surfers Paradise, the heart of the Gold Coast** Surf rolls in from the Pacific Ocean onto long, sandy beaches.

13

THE TROPICAL COAST

The Bruce Highway runs past 900 miles (1,400 kilometers) of sugarcane fields along Queensland's coast. In June, before the cane is cut, the green leaves are burned off. You can see the fires burning against the evening sky. Bundaberg is a town at the southern end of the sugarcane belt. Bundaberg is famous for its rum. This is a strong spirit made from molasses (cane syrup with the sugar taken out). Sea turtles come to lay their eggs on the beach at Bundaberg. Scientists also come here to watch them.

The Bruce Highway ends at Cairns, Australia's most northern city. It first became important in the 1890s, when a railroad was built, linking the coast with the tin mines farther inland. You can still travel on part of that line. It runs through jungle and rugged countryside as far as the little town of Kuranda. The train climbs more than 1,000 feet (300 meters), rounds 98 bends, and crosses many bridges built over steep ravines.

From Cairns, you can take a boat out to the Great Barrier Reef. Hundreds of reefs and islands make up the Great Barrier Reef, which stretches for 1,200 miles (1,900 kilometers) down the Australian coast. You will need a snorkel, goggles, and fins to explore this underwater paradise. All kinds of brilliantly colored fish can be seen swimming among fantastic coral clusters. By best count, there are about 1,400 kinds of fish and 300 varieties of coral.

To reach Cape York, the northernmost tip of Australia, you cross some of the roughest country on the continent. The only roads are dirt roads, and these are washed away when it rains. Even when it is dry you need a four-wheel-drive vehicle, and you may have to drive through rivers.

△ **Trinity Wharf, Cairns** Cabin cruisers and yachts line the pier at the marina. On the opposite side of the bay, a tropical rain forest covers the hills.

▷ **The Kuranda railway** The thrilling 21-mile (34-kilometer) train ride winds through lush forest and past sheer cliffs and spectacular waterfalls.

▽ **Part of the Great Barrier Reef** A tourist ferry docks alongside a jetty by the reef. Seen from above, the edge of the reef is turquoise and green.

THE TOP END

Fewer people live in the Northern Territory than in any other region of Australia. This vast wilderness stretches from the red desert in the center of the country to the tropical mangrove swamps on the northern coast. About a quarter of the people here are Aborigines. They own nearly half the land.

You can take an airplane from Cairns to Darwin, the capital of the Northern Territory. Darwin is a pleasant town on the tropical northern coast. Australians call this part of the country the "Top End." Here, winters are dry and sunny. But summer brings hot and humid weather with heavy rains. Electric storms light up the skies, and there is a danger of cyclones with their powerful winds. On Christmas Day in 1974, Darwin was flattened by Cyclone Tracy. Much of the town has been rebuilt.

To the east of Darwin is Kakadu National Park. It is one of Australia's great natural attractions. Wetlands and paperbark swamps, eucalyptus forests, and patches of rain forest cover more than 7,000 square miles (20,000 square kilometers). Crocodiles and water birds, such as the red-legged jabiru, live by the rivers, creeks, and lagoons. Dingoes, kangaroos, bats, and many other animals also make their homes in the park. In the wet season, much of the park is flooded. In the dry season, the rangers burn off dry grass to encourage new growth and reduce the risk of a major bush fire later. This activity is a continuation of an ancient custom of the Aborigines, who own and take care of much of the park. At Nourlangie Rock and Ubirr in the east of the park, you can see some fine Aboriginal rock paintings.

▷ **Canoeing through Katherine Gorge, Northern Territory**
For seven miles (twelve kilometers) the Katherine River is lined by red-ochre-colored cliffs.

▷ **A "billy tea party"** When people hiking in the bush stop to make tea, they boil the water in a tin container called a *billy*.

▽ **A young Aborigine next to a rock painting** Some Aboriginal paintings in Kakadu National Park are over 20,000 years old.

THE RED CENTER

The great Australian outback is a huge desert deep inside the continent. Right in the center of it is the little town of Alice Springs. From Darwin, you can fly there or you can follow the Stuart Highway south for 950 miles (1,500 kilometers). The scenery changes from forest near the coast to grassland farther inland to dusty, red desert near the center. Here, it can get very hot during the day, but it is freezing at night.

The settlement of Alice Springs grew after a telegraph line was laid to the north of the country in 1872. The old stone telegraph station is now a museum on the outskirts of the modern town. The railroad did not reach here until 1929. Before then, travelers from Adelaide, on the south coast, had to journey the last few hundred miles by camel. Today, there are roads across the outback. Drivers must watch out for kangaroos.

Uluru, formerly known as Ayers Rock, is the world's biggest single rock. It is 1,150 feet (350 meters) high and measures 6 miles (10 kilometers) around. It rises above the scrubland and red desert 275 miles (445 kilometers) southwest of Alice Springs.

◁ **A "flying doctor"** In the outback, doctors often travel by airplane to reach their patients. They receive their instructions over the radio from Alice Springs. And some children in remote areas even get their schooling by radio or satellite.

▷ **Natural Wonder** The land on which this enormous sandstone rock stands was returned to the Aboriginal people in 1985. Its name was officially changed from Ayers Rock to Uluru. It is at least 600 million years old.

◁ **Dingoes on Uluru** The dingo, or wild dog, is found in outback areas. Dingoes kill rabbits and sometimes attack sheep.

Deep into the Territory, you come across the smooth, rounded rocks known as the Olgas. The Aborigines call these rocks Kata Tjuta, meaning "many heads." The rocks are sacred to the Aborigines, who believe that the Rainbow Serpent, a powerful god, lives here in a water hole during the rainy season. Stories about such fantastic creatures are depicted in Aborigine paintings and dances. "Dreamtime," the name given to the time when Aborigines believe the world began, is another common subject of native art and folklore.

WAY OUT WEST

Perth is the capital of the country's biggest state, Western Australia. Sunshine and long, white, sandy beaches help to make Perth a popular summer resort. Here, cool breezes blow off the Indian Ocean, filling the sails of passing yachts. Perth is a modern city on Australia's southwest coast. Three out of every four Western Australians live in Perth or in the neighboring port of Fremantle. King's Park overlooks Perth. In springtime — September to November — King's Park is covered in orchids and other brightly colored wildflowers.

Farther south is "tall timber country." There are forests of jarrah, karri, and other giant eucalyptus trees. Many of the crossties on Australia's railroads are made of the hardwood jarrah. Karri is turned into woodchips for making paper. Fields of wheat stretch from the Rainbow Coast around the old port of Albany as far as the Great Eastern Highway. Along this road, you will find towns that sprang up 100 years ago. In the 1890s people came from all over the world to dig for gold. Many of those towns are now empty ghost towns. Gold is still mined in great quantities at Kalgoorlie.

The scorching highlands of Pilbara lie 625 miles (1,000 kilometers) north of Perth. The highlands are rich in iron ore. Much of the ore is carried by train to the coast and shipped to Japan to be made into steel. At about the same time as the gold rush, there was a "pearl rush" at Broome, a small town on the northwestern coast. Filipinos, Japanese, and others came here to dive for mother-of-pearl shells on the seabed. Broome lies on the edge of the Kimberley, one of Australia's wildest and least explored regions.

▷ **Perth seen from King's Park** Modern skyscrapers dominate the city skyline, but some of Perth's buildings are very old. Government House was built by convicts in the 1850s.

◁ **Iron ore mining in the Pilbara** Every day, giant earth-moving machines dig out 24,000 tons of rock. Temperatures here often reach 120°F (49°C).

△ **Pelicans on the beach at Monkey Mia, Western Australia** Here, many animals are used to people. Dolphins swim into shallow water where people are waiting to pet them.

GOING SOUTH

The train journey from Perth to the nearest city, Adelaide, takes about two days. The railroad crosses the Nullarbor Plain, a vast desert. The train travels over the world's longest stretch of straight track. The famous Indian-Pacific Railroad, which runs from coast to coast between Sydney and Perth, uses this line.

Adelaide is the pretty capital of the state of South Australia. The well-planned city is surrounded by parks, gardens, and rolling hills. Every year Adelaide hosts a major International Arts Festival.

Driving about an hour from the city of Adelaide will bring you to the Barossa Valley. Some of Australia's best wines are produced here. The valley's first vines were planted by German settlers in the 1840s.

More wine comes from the Riverland towns. These towns are built on land irrigated by the Murray River. The oldest is Renmark. Here, in 1887, water was pumped from the Murray to make the dry soil fertile for the first time. You can still see one of the original wood-burning irrigation pumps in the town.

△ **Adelaide by night** The Torrens River runs through the city. Most of the buildings, old and new, are made of stone quarried nearby.

Paddle steamers once carried cattle and sheep to market down the Murray River. The steamers still cruise downriver, but now they carry tourists. Some of the riverside towns you pass through, with their docks standing high out of the water, look as they did in the old riverboat days.

Far away in the South Australian outback, tall pink slag heaps overlook the Coober Pedy opal mines. Opal is a valuable stone that is made into jewelry. Here, the weather gets so hot that not only the mines, but also the houses, are underground.

△ **"Little Sahara" on Kangaroo Island, South Australia** Large white sand dunes are on the south side of the island. Sometimes whales swim near the island.

◁ **Once popular camel-trekking** Because of environmental damage, this activity no longer occurs on Kangaroo Island. Many kangaroos, wallabies, koalas, platypuses, seals, sea lions, penguins, and a million sheep live on the island.

CITY OF GOLD

Melbourne is a city of tree-lined streets, rattling streetcars, called trams, and sidewalk cafés. With three million people, it is the second largest Australian city. Melbourne is the capital of Victoria, one of Australia's smallest but most populated states.

Melbourne first became important when gold was discovered in the area in the 1850s. Its busy Chinatown district was founded by the Chinese who came from Asia to look for gold and then settled here. Many of the city's fine old buildings were built with money from the goldfields of Victoria. Today the old buildings look small next to the towering modern skyscrapers.

Melbourne's Old Gaol, or jail, once held the notorious "bushranger" Ned Kelly. To the Australians, this outlaw is a folk hero. When he was hanged in 1880, five hundred people gathered here to pay their respects.

△ **Flemington Racecourse, Melbourne** The Melbourne Cup horse race is held here every November. It is a big occasion for the city.

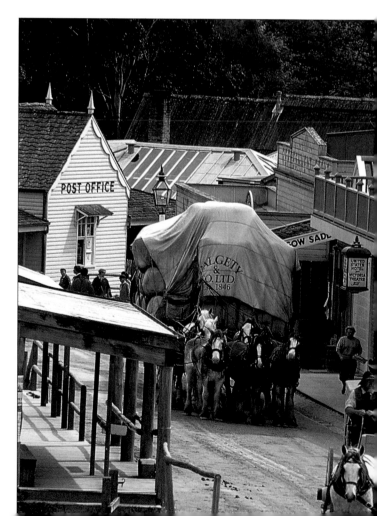

The Melbourne Cricket Ground, the country's biggest sports stadium, holds 100,000 spectators. When the Australian Rules Football championships are held here, the stadium is always full. These games are fast, skillful, and very rough. Players cannot be sent off the field for breaking the rules.

Away from the noise of the city, you can enjoy the peace and beauty of Phillip Island. Here, every day at sunset, hundreds of tiny fairy penguins come out of the water. They waddle across the beach to nest in the sand dunes. To the west of Melbourne are the beautiful Grampian Mountains. You can walk through forests, climb rocks, fish for trout, or admire Aboriginal rock paintings. You may see kangaroos, koalas, echidnas (a type of spiny anteater), or other animals. Hundreds of different kinds of birds live here, including the flightless emu.

◁ **Sovereign Hill Goldmining Town at Ballarat, Victoria** A team of horses pulls a covered wagon along Main Street. Sovereign Hill is a living museum of the old goldmining days. Here, you can ride on a stagecoach, see how the miners lived, and even pan for gold.

▷ **Elizabeth Street, Central Melbourne** The center of the city is a busy place, with people and traffic always on the move. Trams, like the one in the picture, travel all over the city.

THE GREEN ISLAND

Sixteen years after the first European settlers landed in Sydney, a second settlement was begun on the island of Tasmania. The island lies 150 miles (240 kilometers) from the Victoria coast across the Bass Strait. Tasmania is Australia's smallest state.

Tasmania's hills are often covered in mist and rain, and it is cooler here than on the mainland. There are lush green fields, thick forests, and rushing rivers. But the lovely island has a sad history. This was once a convict colony so terrible that prisoners dreaded being sent here. It was even worse for the Aborigines, who were pushed off their lands by settlers.

Tasmania's capital, Hobart, lies on the southeast coast. In the local museum, you can see pictures of the Tasmanian tiger, a striped, doglike animal that once lived on the island but is now extinct. In January, crowds flock to Hobart's harbor to see the finish of the yearly Sydney-to-Hobart yacht race. Restaurants and shops line the harbor. Some of these old buildings were once warehouses where wool and wheat were stored before being shipped abroad.

Most Tasmanians live near the north and southeast coasts. The western side of the island is much wilder. In the Cradle Mountain-Lake St. Clair National Park, you will find rugged mountain scenery. The famous Overland Track through the park is the best "bushwalk" in Australia. The walk takes at least five days to complete. You need a tent for sleeping as well as plenty of food and warm clothing. The weather here can change quickly from sunshine to pouring rain or even snow. Tasmania is different from the rest of Australia, but you will find it just as exciting.

▷ **Hobart and its beautiful harbor, seen from the air** In the background, mountains rise above the city. For two months in winter, the mountains are covered with snow.

◁ **Boats lining the docks in Hobart harbor** Down on the waterfront, you can often buy fresh lobsters directly from the fishing boats.

▷ **Rafting on the Franklin River, Tasmania** A trip down the wild Franklin River, through white water rapids, is a great adventure.

AUSTRALIA FACTS AND FIGURES

People
Most Australians are of European origin. Many are descended from early British and Irish settlers. Others are of Italian, Greek, Turkish, southern Slav, or Lebanese origin. There are also Asians, including Vietnamese, Chinese, Thais, Malaysians, and Japanese. Recently, people have come from both South and North America as well as Africa. Aborigines make up about one percent of Australia's population.

Trade and Industry
Australia is very rich in minerals. It is the world's most important producer of bauxite (for making aluminum) and has huge deposits of iron ore. Coal is found in New South Wales and Queensland, and gas and oil are found off the coast of Victoria. Iron and coal are shipped all over the world. One of Australia's biggest customers is Japan. Iron and steel manufacturing are very important industries.

Tourism, especially on the Great Barrier Reef, space communication technology, film making, and wine making are also important industries.

△ **A "road train" and its driver** These huge trucks and their trailers take supplies to the farthest parts of the outback.

Farming
Australia's farms occupy nearly two-thirds of the country. Much of the land is used for grazing sheep and cattle. Sugarcane is grown along the Queensland coast, and wheat in southeast and southwest Australia. Other crops include cotton, sunflower seeds, barley, and rice, cotton, and grapes.

Australia is the world's leading wool producer. The tough merino breed of sheep can be raised in areas where there is little rainfall. Beef cattle are found in New South Wales and Queensland. Dairy cattle, which need more rain, are raised on the New South Wales coast and in southern Victoria. Brahmin cattle are found in the north.

Fishing
Black and blue marlin, mackerel, tuna, barracuda, and saltfish are caught all along the east coast. Barramundi, jacks, and tarpon are found in both fresh and salt water. Rainbow trout live in the lakes and rivers. Australia's fishing fleets trawl the Indian and Pacific Oceans.

Food
Australia has many, many kinds of restaurants. All kinds of Asian food are very popular, but it is possible to eat foods from nearly every country in the world. Seafood is fresh and cheap, so prawns, oysters, scallops, and lobsters, as well as the traditional steak, are often eaten at outdoor barbecues.

Fresh fruits are in abundance— bananas, papayas, mangoes, and pineapples in the north and apples, oranges, peaches, and berry fruits in the south.

Some peculiarly Australian dishes are :
meat pie: cooked meat and dark gravy inside a pastry crust
pavlova: a meringue dessert covered with cream and fruits
lamington: squares of sponge cake dipped in chocolate and coconut

Religion

Australia has no official religion. Most people are Christians. Protestants and Roman Catholics are the biggest groups. Others include members of the Greek and Slavic Orthodox Churches. Islam, Buddhism, and other religions are also practiced.

The Aborigines believe in the Dreamtime. This tells how the world began and of the need for people and nature to be as one.

Schools

Many children in the cities attend nursery school. From the age of five, children must go to school full time until their fifteenth birthday (sixteenth in Tasmania). Many children stay in school for two more years, and then go on to university.

Most schools are run by the state, and education is free. Some are run by religious bodies.

Children who live in the outback and cannot attend school are taught over the radio and by satellite transmission by the School of the Air and other Distance Education facilities. Work is sent to them by mail and delivered by small aircraft.

△ **Surf lifesaving boat** A crew of lifeguards battles its way through the surf. The guards are responsible for the safety of beach users, and they rescue surfers who get into trouble.

The Media

The Australian is Australia's only national daily newspaper. But each state capital publishes its own daily paper. The *Sydney Morning Herald* and Melbourne's *The Age* are sold throughout the country. Magazines include *Time Australia* plus ones about fashion, sport, and many other topics. *Australian Geographic* is devoted to the country's wildlife and environmental issues.

There are five main television channels plus satellite stations and local channels. The national network is the Australian Broadcasting Corporation (ABC). The SBS channel broadcasts in both English and other languages. Radio includes ABC programs and a wide variety of others.

Art and Drama

Some cave paintings by Aborigines are over 20,000 years old. They include hunting scenes showing stick figures painted in red. Later Aboriginal paintings depict fish, turtles, and other animals. Tom Roberts (1856-1931) painted the official picture of the first Australian parliament. Recently, Australian-made films have become popular worldwide.

Literature

Australian literature began with the letters of the early settlers. "Banjo" Paterson (1864-1941), the most famous "bush" poet, wrote *Waltzing Matilda*, Australia's unofficial anthem.

Australian novelists and playwrights often write about their country. Ralph Bolderwood's (1826-1915) novel *Robbery Under Arms* tells the story of an outlaw in the bush. In *The Chant of Jimmy Blacksmith*, Thomas Keneally (1935-) writes about the tragic life of an Aboriginal boy. Aboriginal novelists, such as Faith Bandler and Colin Johnston, have also written about the problems of their people.

AUSTRALIA FACTS AND FIGURES

△ **A baby koala clings to its mother's back**
Koalas live on the east coast of Australia and feed on eucalyptus leaves. When the babies are small, they live in the mother's pouch.

Festivals

All kinds of festivals are held throughout the year. Here are just a few:

January **Festival of Sydney** Free concerts in the park, parades of floats through the city, and ferry racing in the harbor

April **Barossa Valley Vintage Festival** A week of wine tasting, brass bands, and sheepshearing

June **Melbourne International Film Festival** New films shown, prizes awarded to actors and directors

June **Cape York Aboriginal Dance Festival** A celebration of Aboriginal dancing and culture, held every two years

Sports

Australians are great lovers of sports and enjoy spending time outdoors. They swim and go surfing. They play cricket, tennis, golf, rugby, soccer, and netball, which is the country's largest participatory sport. They enjoy sailing, fishing, and other popular water sports.

Australian Rules Football is a popular spectator sport. "Footy," as it is known, is played by two teams of 18 players on a big oval field, using an oval-shaped ball.

Rugby League, also played with an oval ball, is popular in New South Wales and in Queensland.

Cricket is the favorite summer game. Teams from all Australia's states play matches against each other and against touring teams from other countries.

Australia is one of the few countries that has participated in every Olympic Games.

Plants

Forests are found mainly on the north and east coasts. The most common trees are eucalyptus — or gum — trees and wattles, or acacia. Mangrove swamps are found on the tropical coasts. In the drier regions, grassland gives way to mallee scrub and spinifex, or porcupine grass. Desert flowers can suddenly bloom for a short time after rain. Native wildflowers are plentiful in Western Australia.

Animals

Kangaroos, wallabies, koalas, and wombats are among Australia's marsupials. (The young develop in the mother's pouch.) The duck-billed platypus and echidna are the world's only mammals that lay eggs. Australia has thousands of kinds of birds, including emu and kookaburra. Some Australian snakes are deadly. The estuarine crocodile is big and dangerous.

Poisonous spiders include the funnel web, found in and around Sydney, and the redback. The sting of the box jellyfish, found in the ocean, is also highly poisonous.

HISTORY

The first people to live in Australia may have come from Asia more than 40,000 years ago. They were the Aborigines, who lived by hunting.

In the 1600s, Dutch explorers sailed around Australia but did not stay. The English explorer James Cook landed at Botany Bay in 1770 and claimed the east coast of Australia for Britain. The British decided to send prisoners there, and in 1788 the first convict ships arrived in Sydney Harbor. Other ships full of convicts and free settlers soon followed. The continent was divided into six states and two territories.

From the early 1800s, large numbers of sheep were brought to Australia. Farmers in search of grazing land for their flocks drove the Aborigines from their traditional hunting grounds. Many Aborigines were killed or died of hunger.

In 1851, gold was discovered, and people came from Europe, the United States, and China to join the gold rush. But by 1900, the gold boom was over.

In 1901, the states formed a Commonwealth with its own parliament led by a prime minister and a group of advisors.

During the two World Wars, Australians fought alongside the British and other Allies. Since then, Australia has cut some of its ties with Britain and looked to Asia and the countries of the Pacific as trading partners.

In 1967, the Aborigines were, for the first time, given the right to vote in elections. Later they were given back the rights to some of their traditional lands.

LANGUAGE

The official language of Australia is English, but other languages are spoken, including Greek, Italian, Arabic, Vietnamese, Chinese, and Slavic languages. Most of the 250 or so Aboriginal languages are now dying out.

Australian English, or "Strine," developed from English spoken by early settlers. It includes some words from Aboriginal languages. The Australian accent flattens the sound of many words, and long words often get shortened in informal situations. Accents vary slightly from state to state.

English	"Strine"
an Australian	Aussie
barbecue	barby
water hole	billabong
can for boiling water	billy
man, guy	bloke
terrific	bonzer
wild countryside	bush
outlaw, bandit	bushranger
ill, broken	crook
real, genuine	dinky-di
foolish person	drongo
honest	fair dinkum
hello, hi	G'day

English	"Strine"
get angry	go crook
make a fuss	go off like a bucket of prawns in the sun
well done	good on yer
tired	knackered
friend, buddy	mate
remote part of Australia	outback
Australia	Oz
I think	reckon
kangaroo	roo
day off work	sickie
bedroll	swag
complain	whinge

INDEX

Acknowledgments
Book created for Highlights for Children, Inc. by Bender Richardson White.
Editors: Peter MacDonald and Lionel Bender
Designer: Malcolm Smythe
Art Editor: Ben White
Editorial Assistant: Madeleine Samuel
Picture Researcher: Annabel Ossel
Production: Kim Richardson

Maps produced by Oxford Cartographers, England.
Banknotes from Thomas Cook Currency Services.
Stamps from Stanley Gibbons.

Editorial Consultant: Andrew Gutelle
Australia Consultant: Denise Ryan, Victoria
Managing Editor, Highlights New Products: Margie Hayes Richmond

Picture credits
EU = Eye Ubiquitous, WPA = Wildlight Photo Agency. Z = Zefa. t = top, b = bottom, l = left, r = right.
Cover: Z. Page 6: APL/Z. 7t: EU/J. Winkley. 7b: Z. 8tr: EU/A. Carroll. 8b: Philip Quirk/WPA. 9: Peter Soulness/WPA. 10l: Z. 10r: Grenville Turner/WPA. 11: Philip Quirk/WPA. 12l: EU/David Moore. 12b: Z. 13t: EU/J. Winkley. 14, 15b: Z. 15t: Grenville Turner/WPA. 16-17: EU/David Batterbury. 17t: EU/Bennett Dean. 17b: EU/John Miles. 18: Grenville Turner/WPA. 19t: APL/Z. 19b: Z.20-21: EU/David Batterbury. 21t: Z. 21b: EU/Paul Bennett. 22l: Philip Quirk/WPA. 22-23, 23tr: David Witts/WPA. 24l: Philip Quirk/WPA. 24r: Carolyn Johns/WPA. 25: Paul Thompson/EU. 26-27b: Philip Quirk/WPA. 26t: Bjørnar Johansen/DAS Photographs. 27t: Peter Solness/WPA. 28: EU/Bennett Dean. 29: Z. 30: Z. *Illustration on page 1* by Tom Powers.